At the Beach

Shira Evans

Washington, D.C.

Vocabulary Tree

The beach

Things at the beach	How the beach looks
sand	sandy
crabs	white
shells	dark
tide	rocky
tide pools	smooth
sea stars	

The beach is by the ocean.
It's sandy.

Some beaches have white sand.

Some beaches have dark sand.

Some beaches are rocky.

Some beaches are smooth.

Crabs live at the beach.

Some beaches have big crabs.

Some beaches have small crabs.

There are different shells

on the beach, too.

The beach keeps changing.
The tide can be high.

Or it can be low.

When it's high tide, there is a lot of water.

When it's low tide, there is less water.

Some beaches have tide pools

when it's low tide.

In a tide pool, you can see sea stars

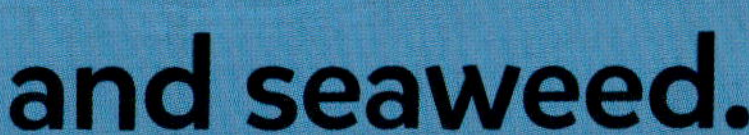

and seaweed.

Soon it will be high tide, and the beach will change again.

Your Turn!

**Describe each beach.
Use the words below.**

white sand | rocky | tide pool

smooth | dark sand

Random House Children's Books
A division of Penguin Random House LLC
1745 Broadway, New York, NY 10019
penguinrandomhouse.com
rhcbooks.com

Library of Congress Control Number: 2025942150
ISBN 978-1-4263-7816-4 (trade paperback) –
ISBN 978-1-4263-7817-1 (lib. bdg) –
ISBN 979-8-217-22802-7 (ebook)

The works that appear herein were originally published separately in slightly different form as: *At the Beach* by Shira Evans (2017); *Swim, Fish!* by Susan B. Neuman (2014); *Peek, Otter!* by Shira Evans (2016); *Dive, Dolphin!* by Shira Evans (2016); and *Whales* by Jennifer Szymanski (2020).

Manufactured in China
10 9 8 7 6 5 4 3 2 1
First Omnibus Edition

The authorized representative in the EU for product safety and compliance is Penguin Random House Ireland, Morrison Chambers, 32 Nassau Street, Dublin D02 YH68, Ireland, https://eu-contact.penguin.ie.

Random House Children's Books supports the First Amendment and celebrates the right to read.

Designed by Sanjida Rashid and Lauren Sciortino

The publisher gratefully acknowledges the expert literacy review of this book by Kimberly Gillow, Principal, Milan Area Schools, Michigan.

Photo Credits
Cover, Spanishalex/Getty Images; 1, Aliaksandr Mazurkevich/Alamy Stock Photo; 2-3, Matteo Colombo/Getty Images; 4, tommasolizzul/Getty Images; 5, Philip Rosenberg/Getty Images; 6, Ian Trower/AWL Images Ltd/Getty Images; 7, ronniechua/Getty Images; 8-9, Photon-Photos/Getty Images; 10, Morales/Getty Images; 11, Colin Marshall/Minden Pictures; 12-13, Arco Images/Alamy Stock Photo; 14-15, Michael Marten; 16-17, Michael Marten; 18-19, John White Photos/Getty Images; 20, Craig Tuttle/Getty Images; 21, Richard Fairless/Getty Images; 22, Ralph Lee Hopkins/National Geographic Image Collection; 23 (UP LE), danilovi/Getty Images; 23 (UP RT), Michael Marfell/Getty Images; 23 (LO LE), Sirachai Arunrugstichai/Getty Images; 23 (LO CTR), Colin Monteath/Minden Pictures; 23 (LO RT), Glow Images, Inc/Getty Images; 24, M Swiet Productions/Getty Images

Pre-
reader
Swim, Fish!
Susan B. Neuman
NATIONAL GEOGRAPHIC
Washington, D.C.

Vocabulary Tree

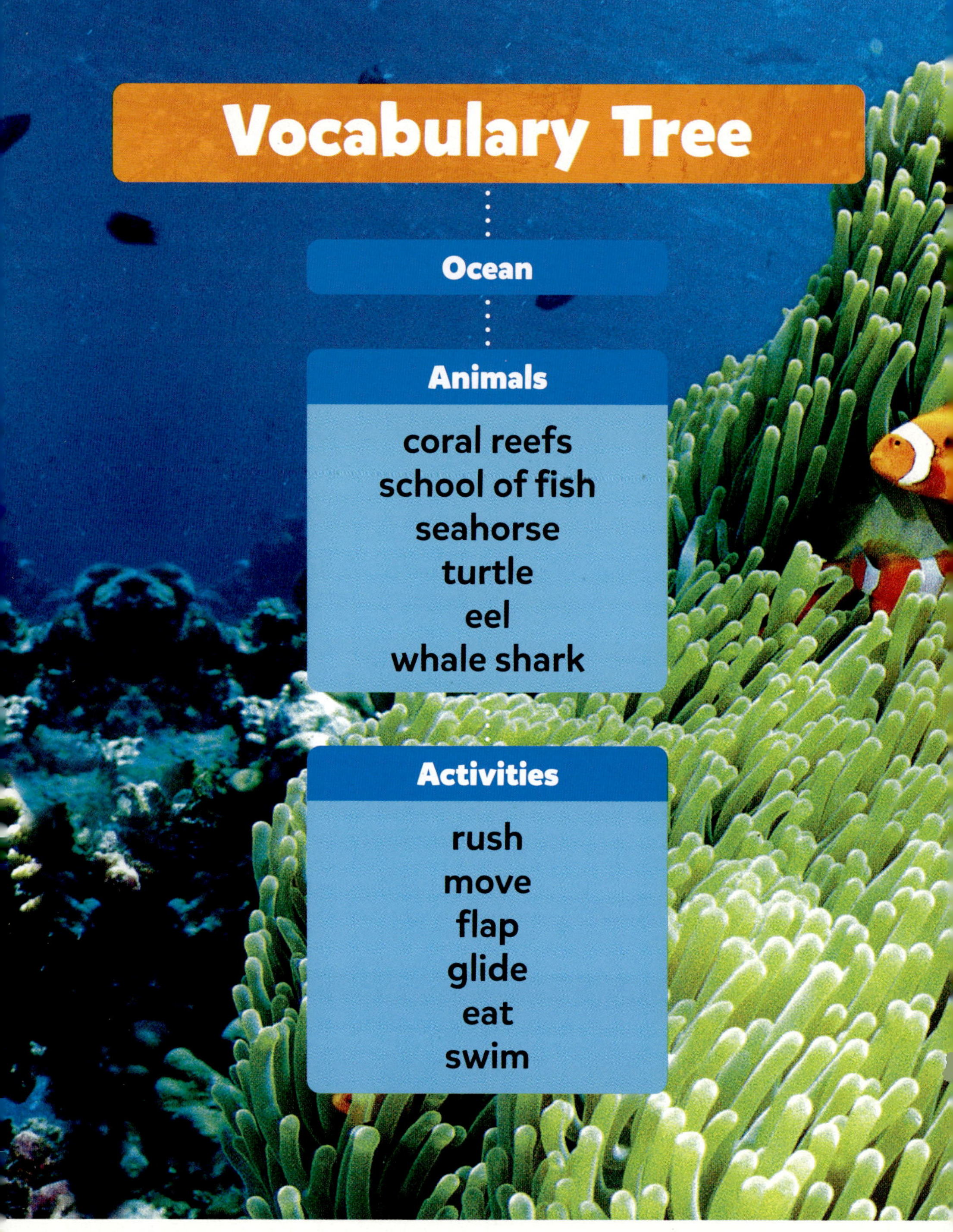

Ocean

Animals

coral reefs
school of fish
seahorse
turtle
eel
whale shark

Activities

rush
move
flap
glide
eat
swim

Let's swim!

Follow the fish to a coral reef.

The water here is warm.

Corals grow.
They make big reefs.

Schools of fish

sergeant majors

rush back and forth.

Seahorses move

up and down and sideways.

Turtles flap their flippers

green sea turtle

like birds flap their wings.

Eels glide from place to place.

giant moray eel

Nearby, whale sharks

eat tiny fish.

Some animals here

cushion sea stars

swim very, very slowly.

Some swim very, very fast.

Swim, fish!

These animals live underwater.

The ocean is their home.

Coral Reef Map

Coral reefs are found all over the world. See where corals and their animal neighbors live.

Your Turn!

Which animals live in a coral reef?

The answer is on the next page.

Designed by David M. Seager and Lauren Sciortino

Photo and Map Credits
Cover, Stephen Frink Collection/Alamy; 1, Georgette Douwma/Photographer's Choice RF/Getty Images; 2-3, Chris Newbert/Minden Pictures; 4-5, Georgette Douwma/Photographer's Choice RF/Getty Images; 6-7, Vilainecrevette/Shutterstock; 8-9, Georgette Douwma/Photographer's Choice RF/Getty Images; 10-11, David B. Fleetham/Blue Planet Archive; 12-13, Reinhard Dirscherl/WaterFrame RM/Getty Images; 14-15, Andy Rouse/npl/Minden Pictures; 16-17, Vilainecrevette/Shutterstock; 18-19, Off Axis Production/Shutterstock; 20-21, Brandon Cole; 22, Coral reef data provided by UNEP_WCMC; map by Carl Mehler and Greg Ugiansky; 23 (turtle), James D. Watt/Blue Planet Archive; 23 (angelfish), Georgette Douwma/Photographer's Choice/Getty Images; 23 (clownfish), Gerald Nowak/StockImage/Getty Images; 23 (puppy), AnetaPics/Shutterstock; 23 (bird), Nejron Photo/Shutterstock; 23 (orangutan), Kjersti Joergensen/Shutterstock; 23 (coral reef), Dudarev Mikhail/Shutterstock; 24, Birgitte Wilms/Minden Pictures

Did you find them all?

Peek, Otter!

Shira Evans

Washington, D.C.

Vocabulary Tree

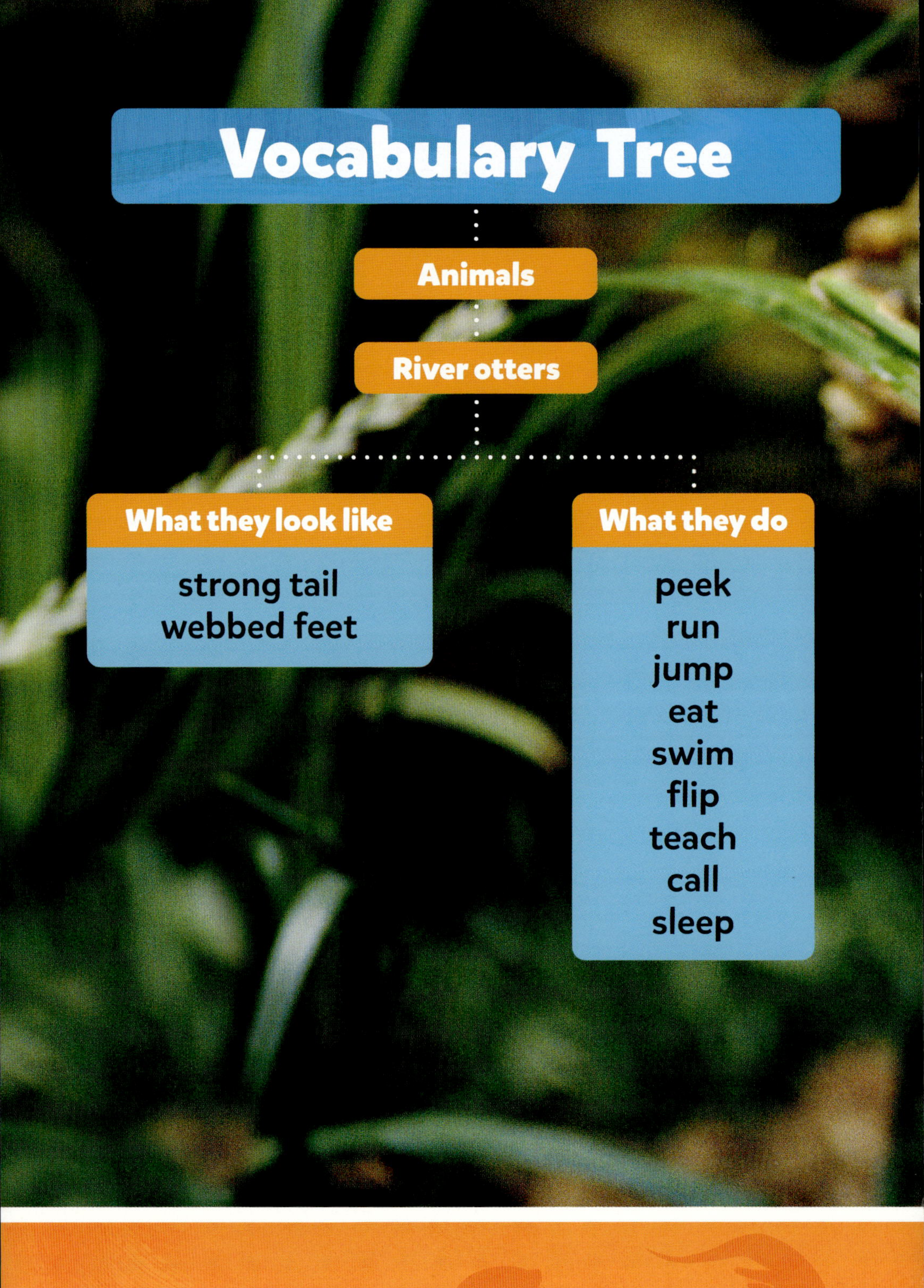

Animals

River otters

What they look like	What they do
strong tail webbed feet	peek run jump eat swim flip teach call sleep

Peek, otter!

Run to the river.

Jump!

What's in the river?

Fish

and crabs.

Eat!

An otter has a strong tail.

It has webbed feet.

Swim! Flip!

This otter teaches its baby to find food.

This otter calls out to its baby.
Where is it?

Here it is!

It's been a busy day.

Sleep, otter!

Your Turn!

Otters teach their babies new things. Adults teach kids new things, too. What are these kids learning?

The answers are on the next page.

Designed by Gustavo Tello and Lauren Sciortino

The publisher gratefully acknowledges the expert literacy review of this book by Susan B. Neuman, Ph.D., professor of early childhood and literacy education, New York University.

Photo Credits
Cover, Andy Rouse/Nature Picture Library; 1, F1online digitale Bildagentur GmbH/Alamy Stock Photo; 2-3, Gerard Lacz/Kimball Stock; 4, Andy Rouse/Nature Picture Library; 5, Andy Rouse/Nature Picture Library; 6-7, Elliott Neep/Minden Pictures; 8, Volodymyr Melnyk/Alamy Stock Photo; 9, Visuals Unlimited, Inc./Fabio Pupin/Getty Images; 10, Louis-Marie Preau/Getty Images; 12, David Tipling/Minden Pictures; 13, Marc Chamberlain/Blue Planet Archive; 14-15, Luciano Candisani/Minden Pictures; 16, Arco Images GmbH/Alamy Stock Photo; 18, David & Micha Sheldon/Getty Images; 19, Chris Reynolds/Alamy Stock Photo; 20-21, F1online digitale Bilda-gentur GmbH/Alamy Stock Photo; 22, S.Cooper Digital/Shutterstock; 23 (UP), blue jean images/Getty Images; 23 (UP CTR), Ronnie Kaufman/Larry Hirshowitz/Getty Images; 23 (CTR), West-end61/Getty Images; 23 (LO), KidStock/Getty Images; 24 (UP), Arco Images GmbH/Alamy Stock Photo

ANSWERS:

1. How to eat
2. How to read
3. How to play ball
4. How to ride a bike

Dive, Dolphin!

Shira Evans

NATIONAL GEOGRAPHIC

Washington, D.C.

Vocabulary Tree

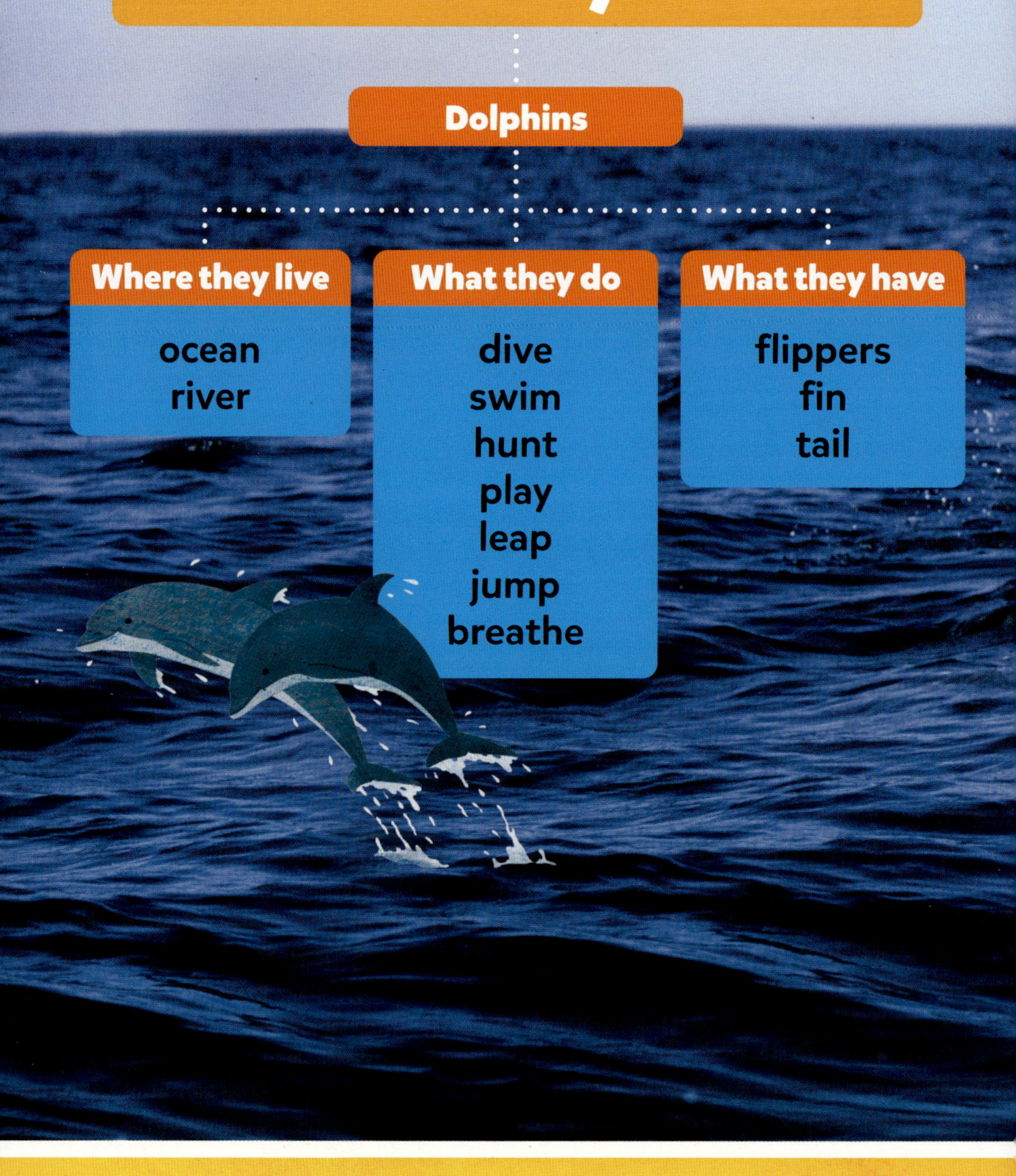

Dive, dolphin!

There are many kinds of dolphins. Some have long beaks.

Some have short beaks.

These dolphins have stripes.

This dolphin has spots.

Some dolphins live in oceans.

Others live in rivers.

fin
tail

All dolphins have
flippers, a fin, and a tail.

Dolphins swim together.

They work as a team to hunt fish.

Dolphins like to play with things they find in the water.

This dolphin plays with seaweed.

They also like to leap and jump.

Dolphins need to breathe.

They come to the top of the water to get air.

Dive, dolphin!

Dolphin Habitat Map

Dolphins live in oceans and rivers around the world. Here's where these dolphins live.

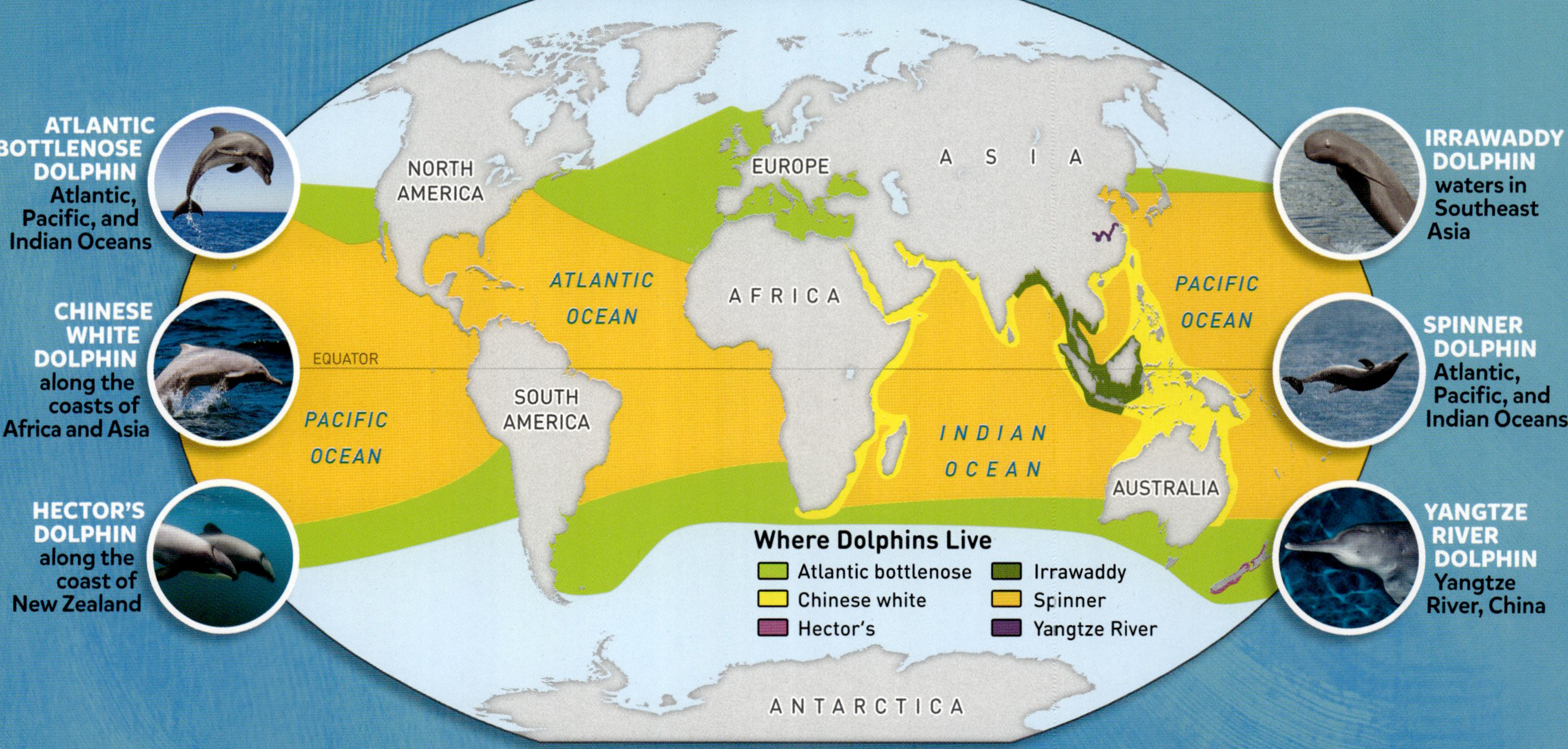

Your Turn!

Match the word to the photo. Use your finger to make a line from the word to the photo.

play

jump

hunt

breathe

The answer is on the next page.

Designed by Rachel Kenny and Lauren Sciortino

The publisher gratefully acknowledges the expert literacy review of this book by Susan B. Neuman, Ph.D., professor of early childhood and literacy education, New York University.

Photo Credits
Cover, Brandon Cole; 1, Willyam Bradberry/Shutterstock; 2-3, Hiroya Minakuchi/Minden Pictures; 4, Mark Carwardine/Minden Pictures; 5, Greg Boreham (TrekLightly)/Getty Images; 6, Brandon Cole/Kimball Stock; 7, Jim Abernethy/Getty Images; 8, Doug Perrine/Blue Planet Archive; 9, Kevin Schafer/Minden Pictures; 10-11, Jeff Rotman/Getty Images; 12-13, Alexander Safonov/Getty Images; 14-15, Reinhard Dirscherl/Getty Images; 18-19, Flip Nicklin/Minden Pictures; 20-21, Juergen and Christine Sohns/Getty Images; 22 (UP LE), Roland Seitre/Nature Picture Library; 22 (UP CTR), Flip Nicklin/Minden Pictures; 22 (UP RT), Roland Seitre/Minden Pictures; 22 (LO LE), Mike Hill/Getty Images; 22 (LO CTR), Thomas Jefferson/Blue Planet Archive; 22 (LO RT), Tobias Bernhard Raff/Minden Pictures; 23 (UP), Stuart Westmorland/Getty Images; 23 (UP CTR), Flip Nicklin/Minden Pictures; 23 (LO CTR), Reinhard Dirscherl/Minden Pictures; 23 (LO), Alexander Safonov/Getty Images; 24 (UP), Jeff Rotman/Getty Images; 24 (inset, UP), Stuart Westmorland/Getty Images; 24 (inset, UP CTR), Flip Nicklin/Minden Pictures; 24 (inset, LO CTR), Reinhard Dirscherl/Minden Pictures; 24 (inset, LO), Alexander Safonov/Getty Images

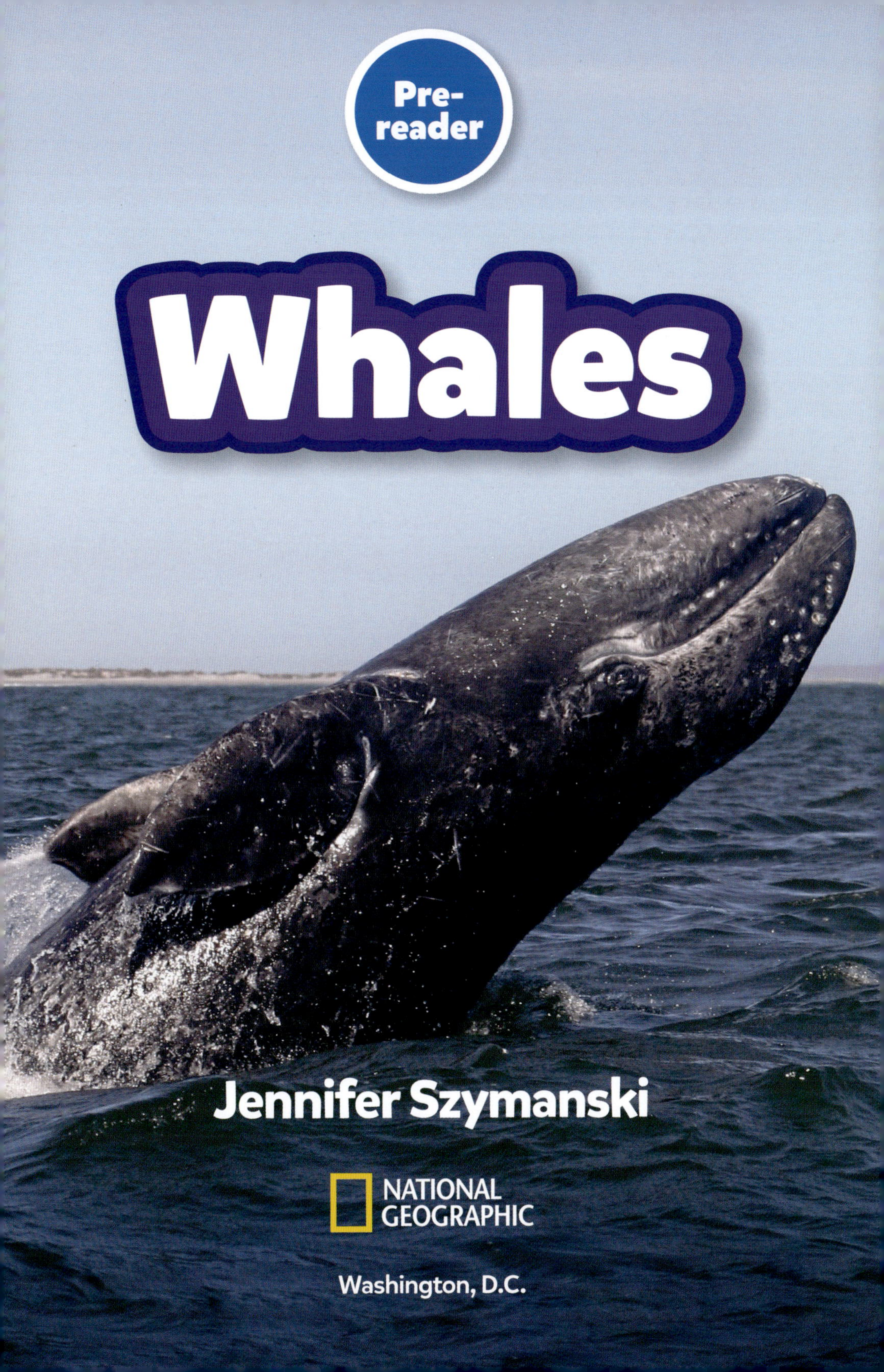

Pre-reader

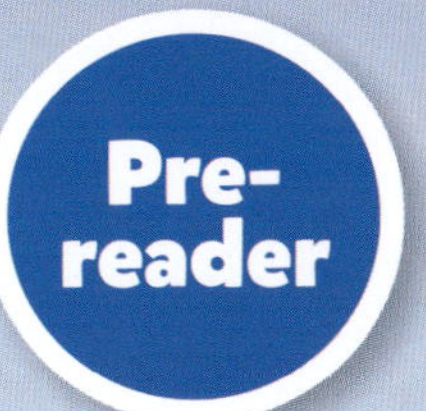

Whales

Jennifer Szymanski

NATIONAL GEOGRAPHIC

Washington, D.C.

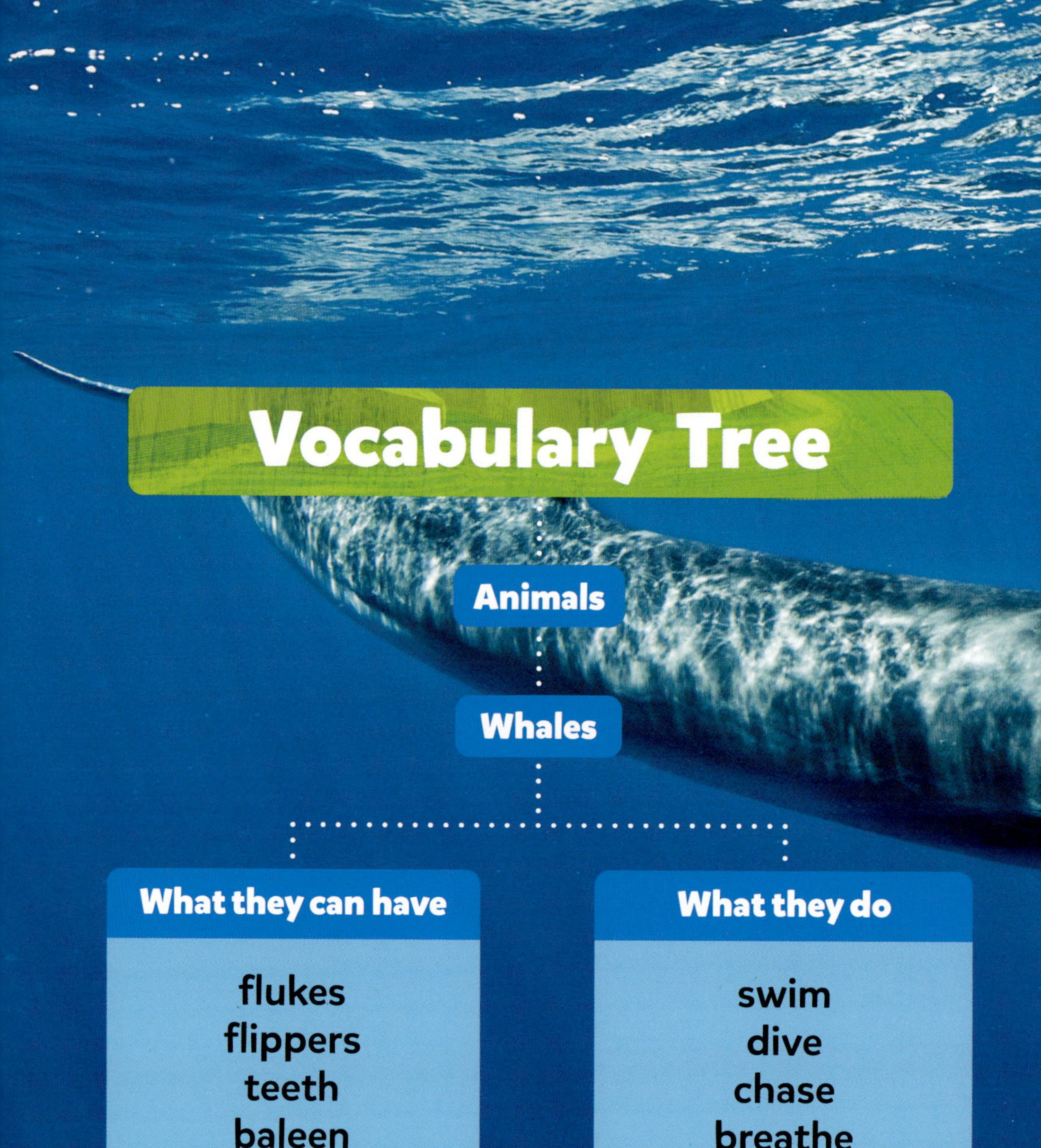

Vocabulary Tree

Animals

Whales

What they can have	What they do
flukes	swim
flippers	dive
teeth	chase
baleen	breathe
blowhole	play

Whales live in the ocean.

Some whales can swim in warm water.

Bryde's whale

Other whales can swim where it is cold.

When some whales dive, their flukes go up.

Then the whale
goes down!

A whale can swim deep in the water.

fin whale

Its flukes and flippers help it move.

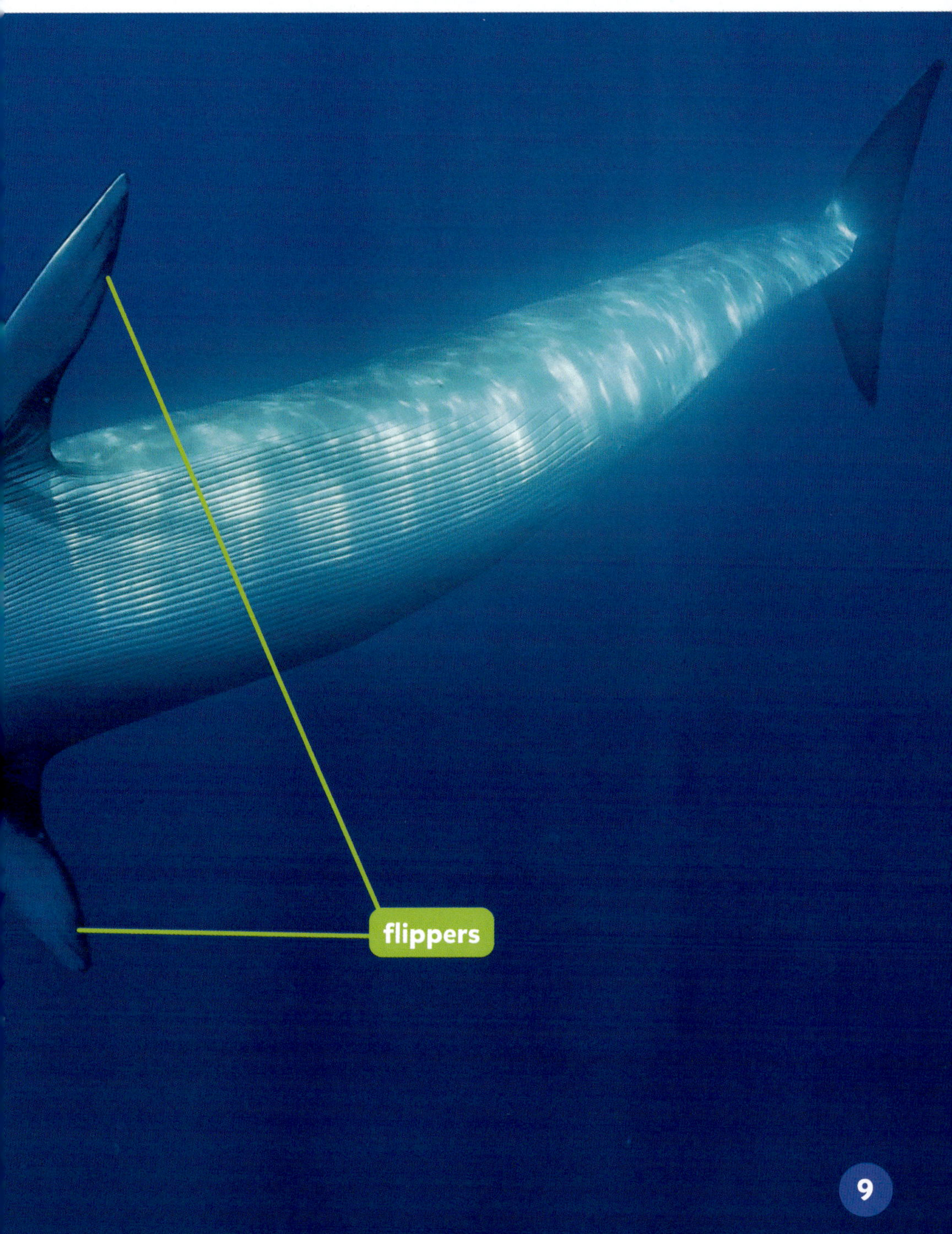

When the flukes go up and down, the whale moves forward.

humpback whales

Its two flippers help the whale turn as it looks for food.

These whales chase food deep in the ocean.

They catch squid and fish with their teeth.

Other whales don't have teeth.
They have baleen (BAY-leen).

Bits of food get trapped on it. Then the whale eats the food.

Blue whales have baleen. They are the world's biggest animals.

But they eat food that is very small!

Time to swim up!
Whales need to breathe air.

humpback whales

Air goes out a whale's blowhole. Then the whale can breathe in.

humpback whales

It's time to play!

Your Turn!

How do baleen whales trap the food they eat? You can find out by doing this easy activity!

What you'll need:

small pieces of paper

a comb or brush

a bowl

water

What to do:

1. Fill the bowl about halfway with water.
2. Sprinkle the pieces of paper on top of the water.
3. Hold the comb or brush so that its teeth or bristles are pointing down.
4. Slowly move the comb or brush through the top of the water.

Did you catch any pieces of paper? If not, try again! Food sticks to a whale's baleen the way paper sticks to your comb or brush. Then—gulp! It swallows its meal!

To Linda, who understands. –J.S.

southern right whales

Designed by Gustavo Tello and Lauren Sciortino

The publisher gratefully acknowledges the expert content review of this book by Dr. Michael Moore, director, Woods Hole Oceanographic Institution Marine Mammal Center, and the expert literacy review of this book by Kimberly Gillow, principal, Chelsea School District, Michigan.

Photo Credits
Cover, by wildestanimal/Getty Images; 1, James Michael Dorsey/Shutterstock; 2-3, Franco Banfi/ Minden Pictures; 4, Doug Perrine/Getty Images; 5, Paul Nicklen/National Geographic Image Collection; 6, James Michael Dorsey/Shutterstock; 7, Michael Nolan/robertharding/Adobe Stock; 8-9, by wildestanimal/Getty Images; 10, WaterFrame/Alamy Stock Photo; 11, romain/Adobe Stock; 12-13, Tony Wu/Nature Picture Library; 13 (INSET), Franco Banfi/Nature Picture Library; 14-15, Christopher Swann/Alamy Stock Photo; 15 (INSET), Mark Carwardine/Getty Images; 16, Richard Herrmann/Minden Pictures; 17, Paul Nicklen/National Geographic Image Collection; 17 (INSET), Tony Wu/Minden Pictures; 18, Michael Nolan/robertharding/Adobe Stock; 20-21, Tony Wu/Nature Picture Library; 22 (UP LE, UP RT, LO LE), Hilary Andrews/NG Staff; 22 (LO RT), violetkaipa/Shutterstock; 23 (UP), Hilary Andrews/NG Staff; 23 (LO), Karen Debler/Alamy Stock Photo; 24, Peter/Adobe Stock